MIGHTY MACHINES

Ambulances

by Kay Manolis

S0-ABA-807

BLASTOFF! READERS

BELLWETHER MEDIA • MINNEAPOLIS, MN

Note to Librarians, Teachers, and Parents:

Blastoff! Readers are carefully developed by literacy experts and combine standards-based content with developmentally appropriate text.

Level 1 provides the most support through repetition of high-frequency words, light text, predictable sentence patterns, and strong visual support.

Level 2 offers early readers a bit more challenge through varied simple sentences, increased text load, and less repetition of high-frequency words.

Level 3 advances early-fluent readers toward fluency through increased text and concept load, less reliance on visuals, longer sentences, and more literary language.

Level 4 builds reading stamina by providing more text per page, increased use of punctuation, greater variation in sentence patterns, and increasingly challenging vocabulary.

Level 5 encourages children to move from "learning to read" to "reading to learn" by providing even more text, varied writing styles, and less familiar topics.

Whichever book is right for your reader, Blastoff! Readers are the perfect books to build confidence and encourage a love of reading that will last a lifetime!

This edition first published in 2008 by Bellwether Media.

No part of this publication may be reproduced in whole or in part without written permission of the publisher. For information regarding permission, write to Bellwether Media Inc., Attention: Permissions Department, Post Office Box 19349, Minneapolis, MN 55419.

Library of Congress Cataloging-in-Publication Data
Manolis, Kay.
  Ambulances / by Kay Manolis.
    p. cm. — (Blastoff! readers) (Mighty machines)
  Includes bibliographical references and index.
Summary: "A basic introduction to ambulances. Simple text and full color photographs. Developed by literacy experts for students in kindergarten through third grade"—Provided by publisher
  ISBN-13: 978-1-60014-176-8 (hardcover : alk. paper)
  ISBN-10: 1-60014-176-5 (hardcover : alk. paper)
  1. Ambulances—Juvenile literature. 2. Ambulance service—Juvenile literature. I. Title.

  TL235.8.M212 2008
  629.222'34—dc22   2007040367

Contents

An Ambulance in Action   4

Parts of an Ambulance   6

An Ambulance at the Hospital   18

Glossary   22

To Learn More   23

Index   24

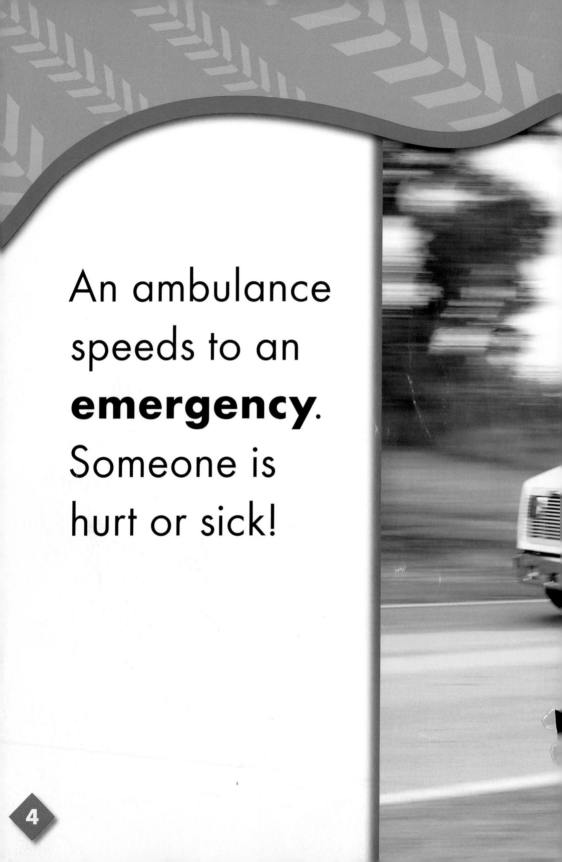

An ambulance speeds to an **emergency**. Someone is hurt or sick!

An ambulance
has flashing
lights and
a **siren**.
These warn
cars to move
to the side.

Wide doors open at the back of the ambulance.

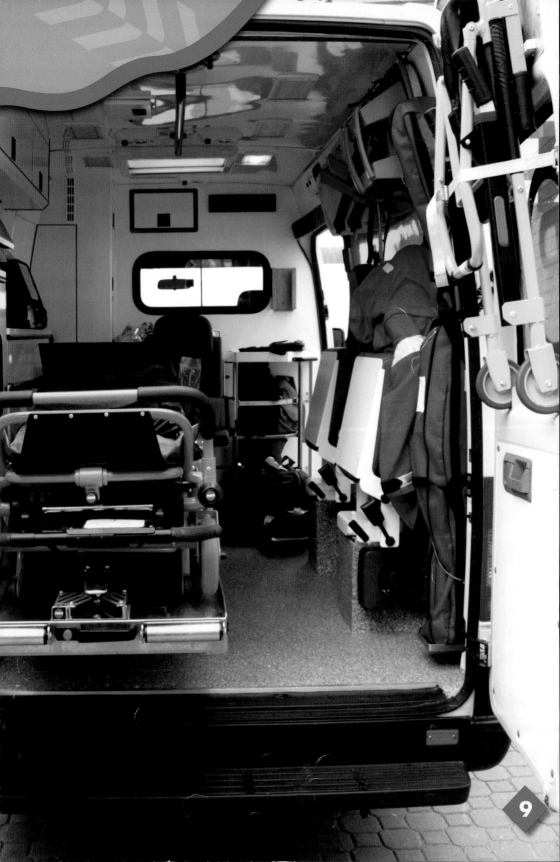

An ambulance carries **medical equipment**. Sick people lie on a **stretcher**.

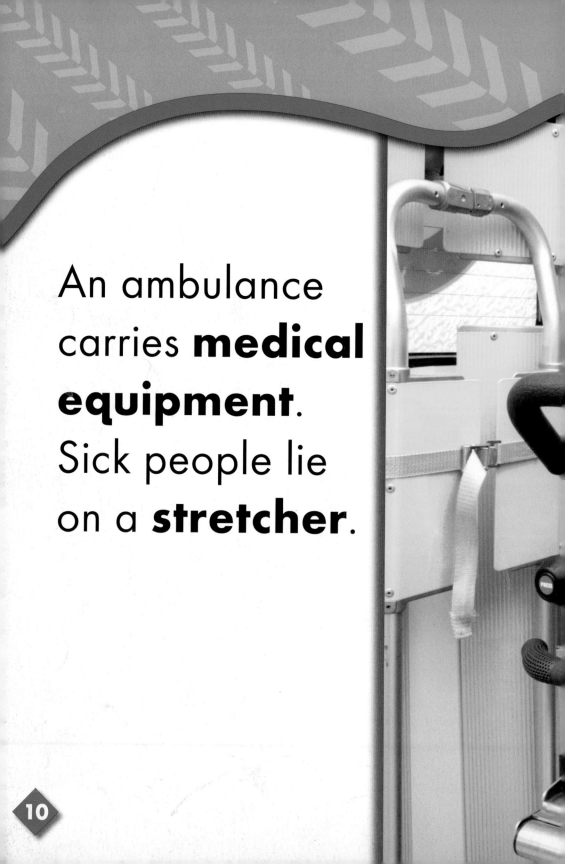

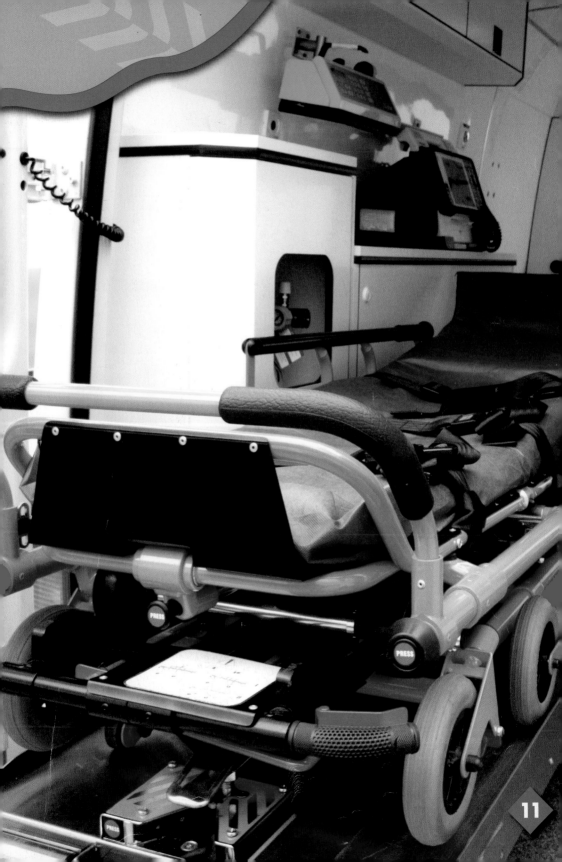

Ambulance workers get to an emergency. They load sick people into the ambulance.

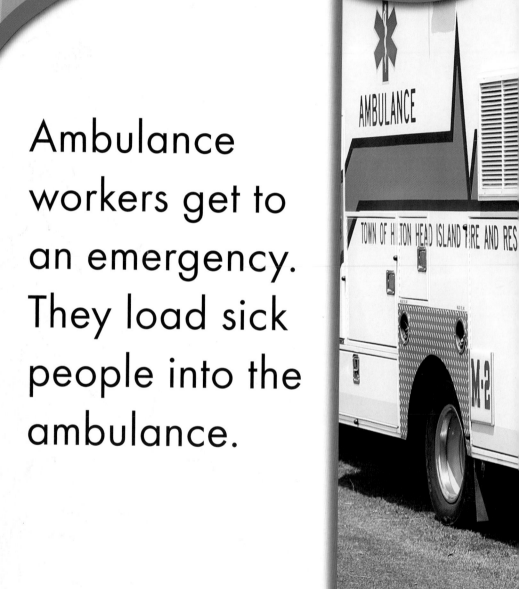

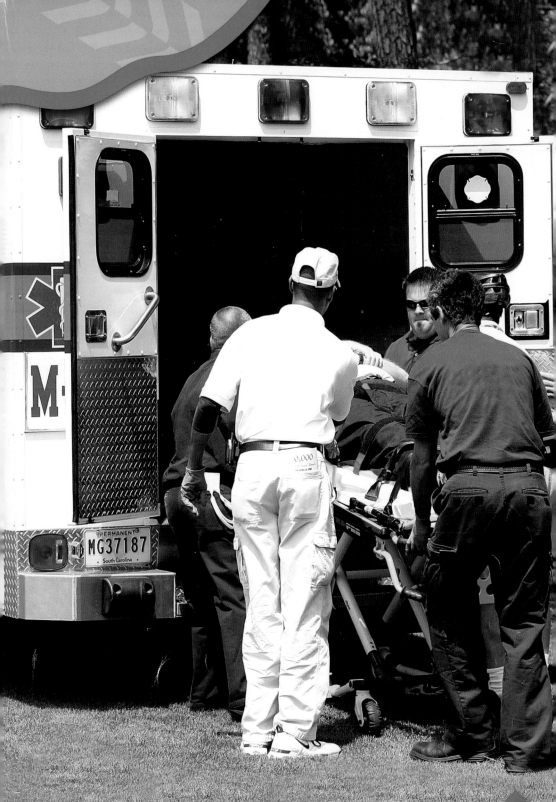

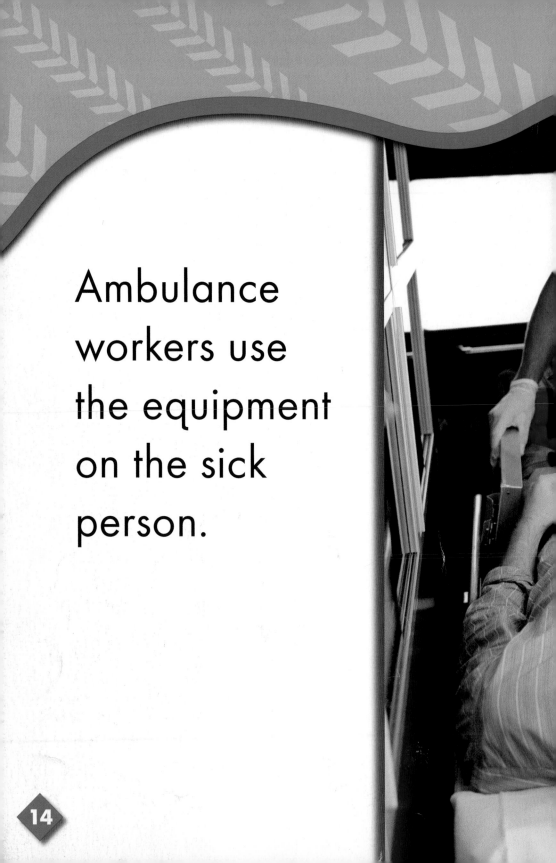

Ambulance workers use the equipment on the sick person.

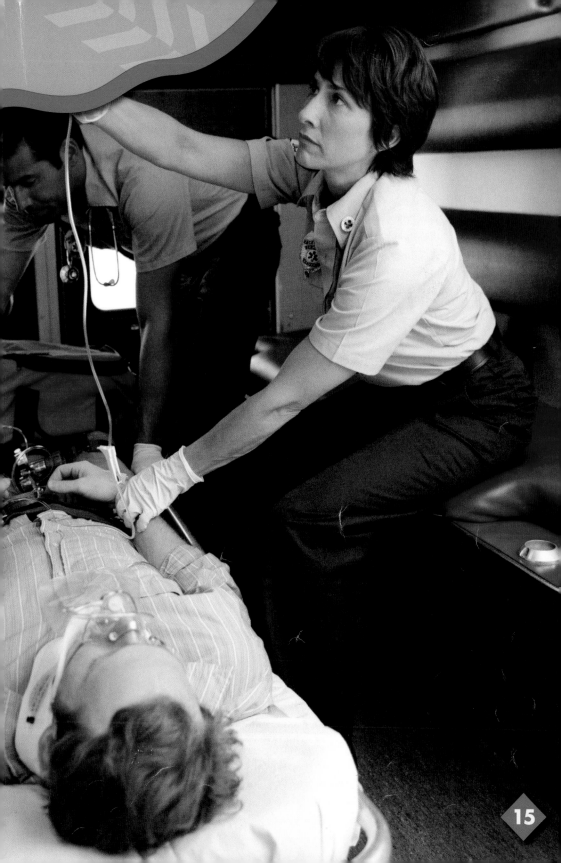

Ambulance workers take care of the sick person on the way to a hospital.

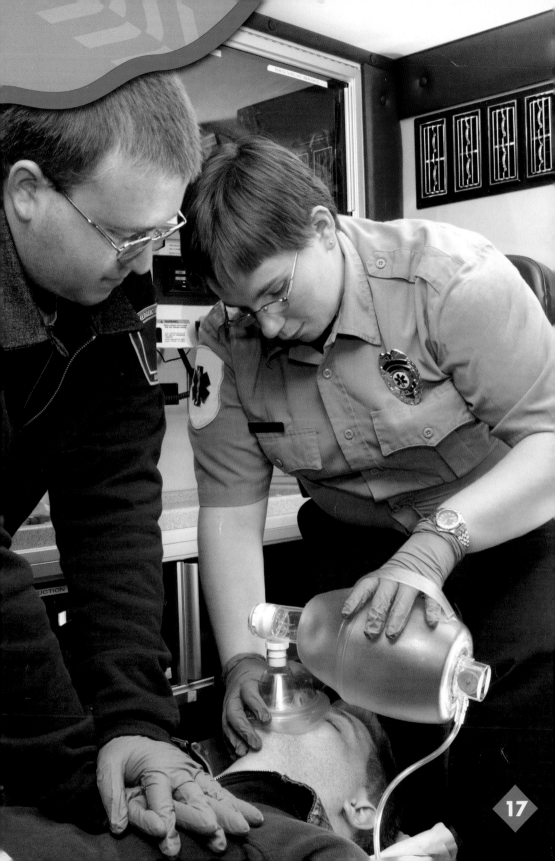

The workers get out at the hospital. They bring the sick person inside.

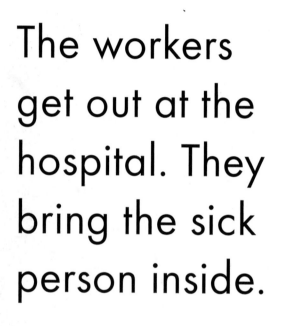

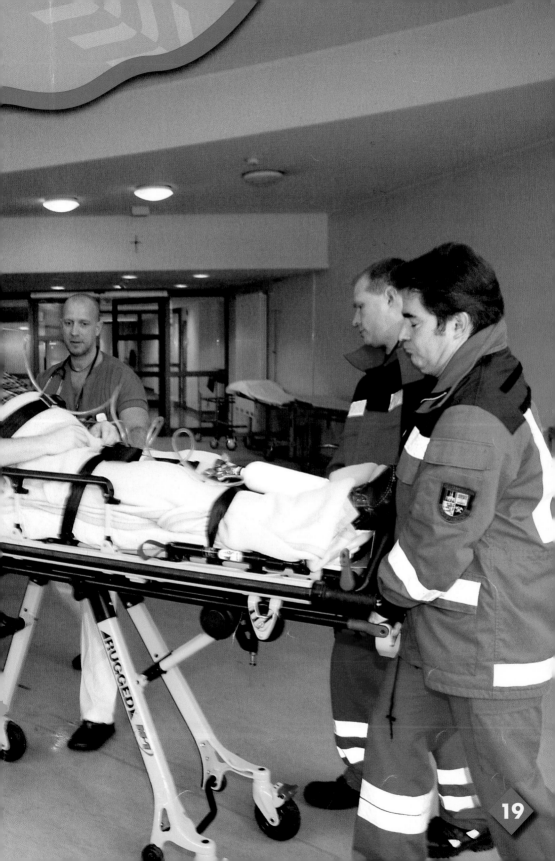

The ambulance
has done
its job.
It is ready
for the next
emergency.

Glossary

emergency—a serious problem or time of danger

medical equipment—things such as bandages and oxygen tanks used when people are sick or hurt

siren—a special horn that makes a loud sound; ambulances use sirens to warn cars that they are coming.

stretcher—a bed that carries a person who is sick or hurt

To Learn More

AT THE LIBRARY

Amoroso, Gary. *Ambulances*. Mankato, Minn.: The Child's World, 2007.

Levine, Michelle. *Ambulances*. Minneapolis, Minn.: Lerner, 2004.

Teitelbaum, Michael. *If I Could Drive an Ambulance!* New York: Scholastic, 2003.

ON THE WEB

Learning more about mighty machines is as easy as 1, 2, 3.

1. Go to www.factsurfer.com

2. Enter "mighty machines" into search box.

3. Click the "Surf" button and you will see a list of related web sites.

With factsurfer.com, finding more information is just a click away.

Index

cars, 6

doors, 8

emergency, 4, 12, 20

hospital, 16, 18

job, 20

lights, 6

medical equipment, 10, 14

people, 10, 12, 14, 16, 18

siren, 6

stretcher, 10

workers, 12, 14, 16, 18

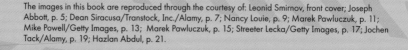

The images in this book are reproduced through the courtesy of: Leonid Smirnov, front cover; Joseph Abbott, p. 5; Dean Siracusa/Transtock, Inc./Alamy, p. 7; Nancy Louie, p. 9; Marek Pawluczuk, p. 11; Mike Powell/Getty Images, p. 13; Marek Pawluczuk, p. 15; Streeter Lecka/Getty Images, p. 17; Jochen Tack/Alamy, p. 19; Hazlan Abdul, p. 21.